W9-AZI-910

To Jane Yolen,
spectacular friend   —L.B.H.

For my father, Dr. Jack Halstead,
who encouraged me in my fascination
with biological science. And for my grandfather,
Jack Halstead, who inspired my interest
in the metaphysical.   —V.H.

Spectacular
Science

A note from the artist: Once I've finished my sketches and done some experimenting to get a sense of what my palette will be, I trace all the sketches onto Strathmore Bristol 500 kid-finish paper. I choose the picture that seems like it would be the most fun to paint and start on that first. This way, I'll be excited to continue with the next one. I work on about four to six paintings at once, adding layer by layer the background, large surfaces, and textures. I use a combination of oil pastels, oil bars, wax, and Prisma color pencils in my art. As each painting dries, I go back into it, adding details, more layers, textures, and then the finishing touches.

First Aladdin Paperbacks edition July 2002

Text copyright © 1999 by Lee Bennett Hopkins

Illustrations copyright © 1999 by Virginia Halstead

ALADDIN PAPERBACKS

An imprint of Simon & Schuster

Children's Publishing Division

1230 Avenue of the Americas

New York, NY 10020

All rights reserved, including the right of

reproduction in whole or in part in any form.

Also available in a Simon & Schuster Books for Young Readers

hardcover edition.

Designed by Heather Wood

The text of this book was set in Cantoria Semibold

Manufactured in China 0916 SCP

20 19 18 17 16 15 14 13

The Library of Congress has cataloged the hardcover edition

as follows:

Spectacular science : a book of poems / selected by Lee Bennett Hopkins ;

illustrated by Virginia Halstead.–1st ed.

p.   cm.

Summary : A collection of poems about science by a variety of poets, including Carl Sandburg,

Valerie Worth, and David McCord.

ISBN 978-0-689-81283-5 (hardcover) 1. Science–Juvenile poetry. 2. Children's poetry, American.

[1. Science–Poetry. 2. American poetry.] I. Hopkins, Lee Bennett. II. Halstead, Virginia, Ill.

PS595.S348S64 1999 811.008'0356–dc21 97-46695 CIP AC

ISBN 978-0-689-85120-9 (Aladdin pbk.)

Page 36 constitutes an extension of this copyright page.

selected by
LEE
BENNETT
HOPKINS

illustrated by
VIRGINIA
HALSTEAD

Spectacular Science

a book of poems

Aladdin Paperbacks
New York London Toronto Sydney Singapore

Contents

What Is Science?

Rebecca Kai Dotlich

What is science?
So many things.

The study of stars—
Saturn's rings.
The study of rocks—
geodes and stones—
dinosaur fossils,
old-chipped bones.
The study of soil,
oil, and gas.
Of sea and sky,
of seed and grass.
Of wind
and hurricanes
that blow;
volcanoes,
tornadoes,
earthquakes,
snow.

What is science?
the study of trees.
Of butterflies
and killer bees.
Glaciers, geysers,
clay, and sand;
mighty mountains,
the rolling land.
The power of trains—
planes that soar.
Science is this
and so much more.
So into the earth
and into the sky;
we question
the how
the where
when
and
why.

Encounter

Lilian Moore

We both stood
heart-stopping
still,

I in the doorway
the deer
near
the old apple tree,

he
muscle wary
straining
to hear

I holding breath
to say
do not fear.

In the silence
between us
my thought said
Stay!

Did it snap
like a twig?
He rose on a curve
and fled.

To Look at Any Thing

John Moffitt

To look at any thing,
If you would know that thing,
You must look at it long:
To look at this green and say,
'I have seen spring in these
Woods,' will not do—you must
Be the thing you see:
You must be the dark snakes of
Stems and ferny plumes of leaves,
You must enter in
To the small silences between
The leaves,
You must take your time
And touch the very peace
They issue from.

The Seed
Aileen Fisher

How does it know,
this little seed,
if it is to grow
to a flower or weed,
if it is to be
a vine or shoot,
or grow to a tree
with a long deep root?
A seed is so small,
where do you suppose
it stores up all
of the things it knows?

Under the Microscope

Lee Bennett Hopkins

Unseen with
an unaided eye
amoebas
glide
on a small
glass slide.

Magnified
one thousand times
protozoans
split in two—

it's miraculous
what
a microscope
can do.

Crystal Vision
Lawrence Schimel

The prism bends a beam of light
And pulls it into colored bands.
My fingers tremble with delight:
I hold a rainbow in my hands.

Magnet

Valerie Worth

This small
Flat horseshoe
Is sold for
A toy: we are
Told that it
Will pick up pins
And it does, time
After time; later
It lies about,
Getting its red
Paint chipped, being
Offered pins less
Often, until at
Last we leave it
Alone: then
It leads its own
Life, trading
Secrets with
The North Pole,
Reading
Invisible messages
From the sun.

Dinosaur Bone

Alice Schertle

Dinosaur bone
alone, alone,
keeping a secret
old as stone

deep in the mud
asleep in the mud
tell me, tell me,
dinosaur bone.

What was the world
when the seas were new
and ferns unfurled
and strange winds blew?

Were the mountains fire?
Were the rivers ice?
Was it mud and mire?
Was it paradise?

How did it smell,
your earth, your sky?
How did you live?
How did you die?

How long have you lain
alone, alone?
Tell me, tell me,
dinosaur bone.

Rocks

Florence Parry Heide

Big rocks into pebbles,
pebbles into sand,
I really hold a million million rocks here in my hand.

Metamorphosis

Carl Sandburg

When water turns ice does it remember
one time it was water?
When ice turns back into water does it
remember it was ice?

How?

Lee Bennett Hopkins

How
do
spiders,
ants,
ladybugs,
bees—

butterflies,
fireflies,
dragonflies,
fleas—

know

to
crawl,
creep,
flit,
flutter,
fly—

as
winter
comes
bitterly
chilling
the
sky?

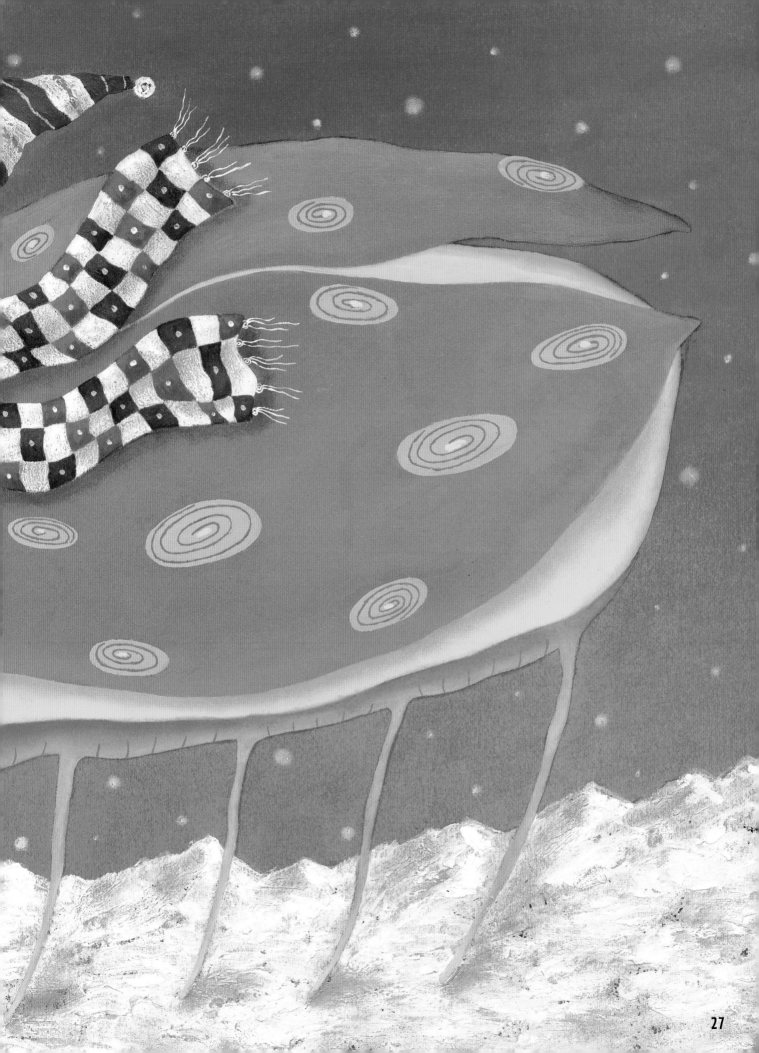

Snowflakes
David McCord

Sometime this winter if you go
To walk in soft new-falling snow
When flakes are big and come down slow

To settle on your sleeve as bright
As stars that couldn't wait for night,
You won't know what you have in sight—

Another world—unless you bring
A magnifying glass. This thing
We call a snowflake is the king

Of crystals. Do you like surprise?
Examine him three times his size:
At first you won't believe your eyes.

Stars look alike, but flakes do not:
No two are the same in all the lot
That you will get in any spot

You chance to be, for every one
Come spinning through the sky has none
But his own window-wings of sun:

Joints, points, and crosses. What could make
Such lacework with no crack or break?
In billions, billions, no mistake?

What Are You, Wind?

Mary O'Neill

What are you, wind?
Only air
Winding in and out of
Everywhere?
If only air,
And thinner than all gauze,
How do you know when
To bluster and to pause?
Or where to go?
How to drift and settle
Each star-flake of snow,
To crest a wave,
Ripple stands of grain,
Make leaves talk
And slant the rain?
What are you, wind
I feel and cannot see,
You, who as breath
Are life itself to me?
How can you slap,
Slam and sting,
Break, destroy, uproot,
And yet so softly sing?
Push at apples
Until they fall,
You with no shape
And no color at all?

Three Skies

Claudia Lewis

Three skies
Above our world—

Grey sky when clouds are high.

Break through the clouds
And it's blue where the planes fly.

Break through the blue on a rocket flight
And the skies are black, day and night.

Break through the black—

Who knows
To what fourth sky,
On what flight?

Stars

Carl Sandburg

The stars are too many to count.
The stars make sixes and sevens.
The stars tell nothing—and everything.
The stars look scattered.
Stars are so far away they never speak
    when spoken to.

Acknowledgments

Thanks are due to the following for works reprinted herein:

Curtis Brown, Ltd. for "How?" by Lee Bennett Hopkins. Copyright © 1992 by Lee Bennett Hopkins; "Under the Microscope" by Lee Bennett Hopkins. Copyright © 1999 by Lee Bennett Hopkins. Both used by permission of Curtis Brown, Ltd. ✳ Rebecca Kai Dotlich for "What Is Science?" Used by permission of the author, who controls all rights. ✳ Farrar, Straus & Giroux, Inc. for "Magnet" from *More Small Poems* by Valerie Worth. Copyright © 1976 by Valerie Worth. Reprinted by permission of Farrar, Straus & Giroux, Inc. ✳ Aileen Fisher for "The Seed" from *Always Wondering* (HarperCollins). Copyright © 1991 by Aileen Fisher. Used by permission of the author, who controls all rights. ✳ Harcourt Brace & Company for "To Look at Any Thing" from *The Living Seed* by John Moffitt. Copyright © 1961 by John Moffitt and renewed 1989 by Henry Moffitt; "Metamorphosis" from *Honey and Salt* by Carl Sandburg. Copyright © 1963 by Carl Sandburg and renewed 1991 by Margaret Sandburg, Helga Sandburg Crile, and Janet Sandburg; "Stars" from *Wind Song* by Carl Sandburg. Copyright © 1960 by Carl Sandburg and renewed 1988 by Margaret Sandburg, Helga Sandburg, and Helga Sandburg Crile. All reprinted by permission of Harcourt Brace & Company. ✳ Florence Parry Heide for "Rocks." Used by permission of the author, who controls all rights. ✳ Claudia Lewis for "Three Skies" from *Poems of Earth and Space* (Dutton). Copyright © 1967 by Claudia Lewis. Little, Brown and Company for "Snowflakes," from *One at a Time* by David McCord. Used by permission of the author, McCord. Used by permission of Little, Brown and Company for "Snowflakes," Morrow & Company. Copyright © 1965, 1966 by David Schertle. Copyright © 1996 by Alice Schertle. Used by permission of Lothrop, Lee and Shepard Books, a division of William Morrow & Company, Inc. for "Dinosaur Bone" from *Keepers* by Alice Begins by Lilian Moore. Copyright © 1975, 1980, 1982 by Lilian Moore; "What Are You, Wind?" from *Winds* by Mary O'Neill. Copyright © 1970 by Mary O'Neill. Copyright renewed 1988 by Erin Baroni and authors. ✳ Marian Reiner for "Encounter" from *Something New* Abagail Hagler. Both reprinted by permission of Marian Reiner for the authors. ✳ Lawrence Schimel for "Crystal Vision." Used by permission of the author, who controls all rights.

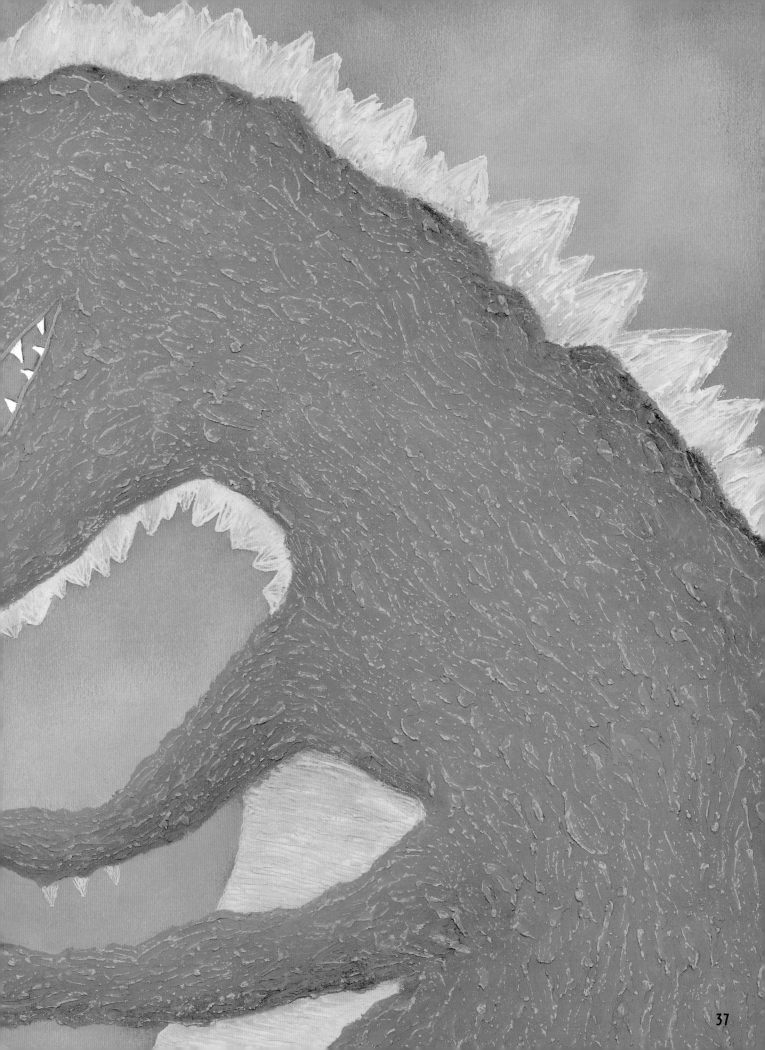